D0526673

YOU CAN FILL A SWIMMING POOL WITH YOUR SPIT!

The fact or fiction behind

HUMAN BODIES

Thurrock Council

3013020877152 6

WAYLAND

Published in paperback in 2014 by Wayland

Copyright © Wayland 2014

Wayland
338 Euston Road
London NW1 3BH

Wayland Australia
Level 17/207 Kent Street
Sydney, NSW 2000

All rights reserved

Editor: Debbie Foy
Design: Rocket Design (East Anglia) Ltd
Illustration: Alan Irvine

British Library Cataloguing in Publication Data
Mason, Paul, 1967-
The fact or fiction behind human bodies. -- (Truth or busted)
1. Human body--Miscellanea--Juvenile literature.
2. Common fallacies--Juvenile literature.
I. Title II. Series
612-dc23

ISBN: 978 0 7502 8158 4

Printed in Great Britain, by CPI Group (UK) Ltd, Croydon, CR0 4YY
10 9 8 7 6 5 4 3 2 1

Wayland is a division of Hachette Children's Books,
an Hachette UK company
www.hachette.co.uk

All illustrations by Shutterstock, except 8, 9, 30, 36, 38, 51, 62, 66, 74

FIND OUT WHETHER YOU SPEND A YEAR OF YOUR LIFE ON THE TOILET...

read on!

Read this bit first...!

Human bodies — we've all got one, but how well do we really understand how they work? Half an hour spent on the internet, or reading those funny emails people send round, reveals all kinds of interesting facts:

'Laughter is the best medicine.'

'Toilet seats are cleaner than computer keyboards.'

'There's enough iron in your body to make an 8cm nail.'

'People fart on average 14 times a day — but more than that if they've been eating beans.'

Are any of these claims actually true, though? In this book we investigate some of the wackiest, strangest, and most surprising myths about the human body.

Some of these facts are actually useful:

⭐ *Do mosquitoes really bite some people and not others and, if so, why?*

⭐ *How much time does each cigarette you smoke take off your life?*

⭐ *Is it actually possible to be scared to death?*

To be honest, though, quite a lot of the facts in **Truth or Busted**'s *You Can Fill A Swimming Pool With Your Spit* aren't particularly useful at all (except for making you look really clever by knowing whether they're true or not). But who wouldn't want to be able to answer questions such as whether you can have brain surgery while you are still awake, does smoking make your teeth fall out, or can chocolate really give you spots?

Finally, this is the place to find out some odd, quirky or just plain revolting things you might never have known about the human body. Examples of these include:

⭐ *Why is poo brown?*

⭐ *Why do older people have big ears?*

⭐ *What actually causes bad breath?*

If this sounds like your kind of thing, **Truth or Busted** is for you!

read on!

So you might hear myths like...

> ## Your body contains enough iron to make a nail

If you've ever accidentally cut your finger and licked away the blood, you'll know that the taste is slightly metallic. But surely that's just a coincidence? Iron belongs in buildings, cars, and machinery — not human bodies!

★ And the truth is...

Your blood *does* have iron in it. The iron has lots of really important jobs, such as helping make new blood cells, getting energy to your muscles, and stopping you from getting ill.

If you could extract all the iron out of your body, there would be enough to make quite a large nail of about 8cm (3in) long. Of course, without the iron doing those important jobs, you'd also start feeling *really* ill, *really* quickly.

Verdict:

TRUTH

I'D NEVER HAVE KNOWN!

Your heart beats so strongly, it could squirt blood up to <u>10 metres</u>!

Your heart's a powerful muscle. Every time it beats, blood surges through your arteries. If your heart was beating quickly, and an artery had a tiny hole in it like the nozzle of a water pistol, blood could squirt a distance of up to 10 metres.

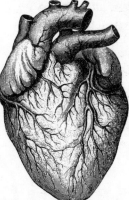

Different areas of your tongue taste different things

This idea has been around for ages (since 1942, in fact). It claims that different tastes are detected by different parts of your tongue. So, for example, the tip of your tongue tastes sweet things. Maybe that's why treats you can lick, like ice creams, toffee apples, and lollipops, are so popular!

If you look in old reference books or on the internet, you'll probably be able to find a drawing of a 'tongue map'. It will likely show sweetness at the tip, bitter tastes at the back, saltiness all over, and sour tastes at the edges.

This tongue map is a joke. But should you take real ones any more seriously?

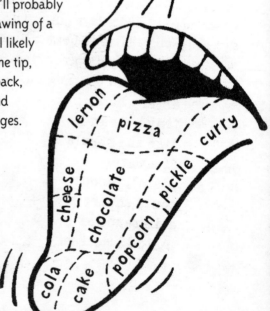

8

A German scientist first put forward the idea that different areas of the tongue tasted food differently in 1901. The theory that some areas were good at sensing particular tastes came later. It was put forward in the 1940s, by a very interesting American researcher named, erm... Edwin Boring.

 The truth is...

There are five different basic tastes: sweet, sour, bitter, salty, and umami (yes, really, umami — it's a taste present in foods such as meat and tomatoes). Every taste sensor on your tongue can actually detect all of these.

> Hmm, that's really umami!

What is true is that some parts of your tongue are better at detecting tastes than others.

(Another odd fact about taste buds is that you lose them with age. By the time you're 60 years old, about half your taste buds will have disappeared!)

Verdict:

Your brain can power a light bulb

Obviously this isn't literally true: where would you plug it in? Your head doesn't come equipped with light bulb sockets. It doesn't even have anywhere to plug in a small table lamp.

Your body does use electricity, though, to pass messages from your brain to other parts of your body and back again. But really — if it were enough to power a light bulb, wouldn't you constantly be getting electric shocks?

⭐ And the truth is...

Your body generates electricity whenever it needs to send messages. Since the brain is your body's control centre, this is where most electricity is generated. There's so much electricity generated by your brain that if you could plug into it, a light bulb would indeed turn on.

The only problem with this would be that without electricity helping control your body's functions, you'd quickly die.

Verdict:  _____ TRUTH _____

10

I'D NEVER HAVE KNOWN!

Here are three more facts about the human brain:

- Messages from your brain to the rest of your body travel at up to 275 kph (170 mph).

- Your brain is more active at night than during the day. When you turn off at night, your brain turns on. Hence all those exciting dreams!

- Because it has no nerve endings or sensory receptors, the brain cannot feel pain! (see page 52).

11

Eating beans make you fart

Parp!

An old rumour says that eating baked beans makes you fart. Maybe you've seen the scene in the old movie *Blazing Saddles*, where a bunch of cowboys are eating beans, then, all of a sudden the inevitable happens?

There's even an old rhyme about beans and their ability to make you pass wind:

> *Beans, beans, the musical fruit,*
> *The more you eat, the more you toot,*
> *The more you toot, the better you feel,*
> *So eat baked beans with every meal.*

★ And the truth is...

Beans contain a special sugar called oligosaccharide. This can't be broken down in the first part of your digestive system, where most food is digested. Instead, the oligosaccharide makes it into the second digestive area, your lower intestine. There, it is a lovely dinner for the bacteria that live there. The only trouble is, those bacteria are the ones that produce fart gas. So... eating beans really does make you fart more.

Verdict:

Here are three amazing facts about the human body:

- Laid flat, the total surface area of your lungs is about the size of a tennis court.

- Laid end to end, the tiny blood vessels of your lungs would stretch 2,400 km (1,491 miles).

- If all the blood vessels in your body were stretched out in a line, the line would be 96,500 km (60,000 miles) long. That's enough to stretch round the entire world two-and-a-bit times!

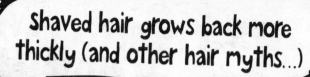

Shaved hair grows back more thickly (and other hair myths...)

We all spend a lot of time thinking about our hair...

'Does this style suit me?'

'Should I have a fringe or not?'

'I wish it were blonde/brown/black/red!'

Is it any wonder that there are so many myths about hair? Here are the most popular:

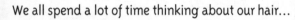

Shaved hair grows back more thickly

It may feel like it, but the truth is that after you shave hair, the blunt, shaved-off ends start to grow out. These are thicker than the ends of hair that have been growing for a while, so shaved areas feel as if the hair's growing back more thickly. It's not, though — in a month's time it will feel just like it always did.

Washing your hair too often makes it fall out

Every time you wash your hair, there's a load of it swirling around the plughole when you finish. Ahh! Shampooing must be making your hair fall out!

In fact, our hair is falling out all the time. Wherever you go you leave a constant trail of hair behind you. But new hair is also growing all the time — so really, there's no need to worry.

Brushing is good for your hair

Girls used to be told that they should brush their hair thoroughly before bed. 'A hundred strokes of the hairbrush before bedtime', grandmas will tell you.

The truth is that brushing isn't very good for your hair, especially hard brushing. It pulls out hair that isn't ready to be shed, breaks hairs, and scratches your head.

Giving your hair a final rinse in lemon juice or vinegar will make it shine

If you're slightly odd and wash your hair with a bar of soap, this is actually true. The acid in lemon or vinegar rinses away the powdery stuff left behind on hair by soap. If you use shampoo, though, this old-fashioned trick won't make your hair any shinier.

You can tell someone's personality from their hair colour

You may hear people commenting on the fact that, say, redheads have terrible tempers; dark, thick hair is a sign of great energy; or blondes have weak personalities. There's literally no evidence that any of these are true!

Verdict: all **BUSTED**

Bleugh

One in every **2,000 babies** is born with a tooth showing. If the tooth is membranous, it will be reabsorbed into the body.

If the tooth is fixed firmly in place but comes out later, no other tooth will replace it until permanent teeth start to appear, at the age of six or seven.

Your hair will live forever

In the British Museum in London, there's a wig from Ancient Egypt. It's curly on top and has long, thin bits dangling down the sides. It's not *quite* today's top style, but back then wigs like this one were all the rage.

The amazing facts about this wig, though, are:

★ **It's 3,500 years old.**

★ **It's made of human hair.**

Hair even older than this has been found in tombs around the world. So, long after the rest of you has disappeared, will your hair still be hanging around?

 And the truth is...

Human hair is practically indestructible, unless you burn it. This is because the only living part of your hair is the tiny bit under your skin. All the rest is dead. There's nothing to interest the bacteria that break up most of the rest of a dead body, so the hair gets left alone.

hair lasts thousands of years, but it's not actually indestructible, so...

Verdict: — **BUSTED**

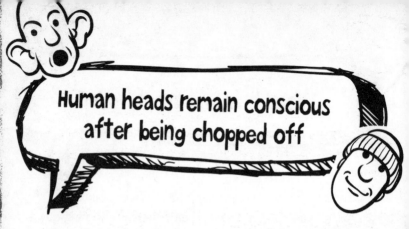

Human heads remain conscious after being chopped off

You'd probably think that having your head chopped off is a pretty decisive way of becoming, well, dead. And yet history is littered with examples of people who had their head chopped off, but appeared NOT to be dead at all for quite some time afterwards...

1. Charlotte Corday, 1793

Charlotte Corday was executed in Paris, France, after she had stabbed to death a man named Marat. Marat was a hero of the French Revolution, which was in full swing at the time. The angry revolutionaries used their new toy, the guillotine, to chop off Corday's head. Then the executioner picked up the head and Corday's eyes are said to have looked at the executioner, while her expression changed to one of extreme annoyance.

2. Antoine Lavoisier, 1794

Once the French revolutionaries got going, they just couldn't stop beheading people using their guillotine. By 1794 they'd started on the scientists, including the famous chemist Antoine Lavoisier. Knowing he was going to die, Lavoisier is said to have

asked his assistant to watch his face after his head had been chopped off. Lavoisier planned to keep blinking for as long as possible. The assistant counted 15 or 20 blinks before Lavoisier finally lost consciousness.

3. Monsieur Henri Languille, 1905

Languille's execution was witnessed by a doctor. The doctor noticed that after his head had been chopped off, Languille's eyelids fluttered and his lips twitched. Even more freaky, when the doctor called his name, Languille's eyes opened. This happened twice in a row, before Languille finally stopped noticing. Presumably he was either dead, or tired of being bothered by someone he didn't even know.

⭐ And the truth is...

Today, most doctors think that it is possible for muscles to keep moving for a short time after death. This does not mean, though, that the brain is controlling the movement. As soon as its supply of blood and oxygen is cut off, the brain starts to die. The process takes no more than two or three seconds.

Verdict: — **BUSTED** —

The acid in your stomach is strong enough to dissolve metal

KLANG!

CRASH!

First of all: do NOT actually try eating any kind of metal to test if this theory is true!

But, in theory, is your stomach acid really so strong it could dissolve metal?

And the truth is...

Your stomach acid helps break down your food so that nutrients can be absorbed into your body. The acid is so strong that it would indeed be able to dissolve a small metal object. So how come your stomach acid doesn't dissolve YOU? There is a strong mucous lining that helps prevent the stomach acid from dissolving you from the inside!

Verdict:  but DON'T try this at home!

TRUTH

Poo can be worth
a lot of money

If this saying really is true,
perhaps we should all think
carefully before flushing the
toilet next time?

 And the truth is...

Poo *can* be valuable. Hundreds of years ago, 'night-soil men' used to collect it for use as a fertilizer, to feed plants. (What a job!) Of course, this doesn't happen any more... but poo can still be worth a lot of money.

In the 1960s, an annoyed Italian artist called Piero Manzoni had an exhibition of cans of his own poo. (Canning poo — another great job!) It was supposed to be a comment on how stupid the art world could sometimes be.

As if to prove Manzoni right, in 2002 a famous London art gallery paid £22,300 for a single can of his poo.

Verdict: _Odd, but... **TRUTH**_

All babies have blue eyes

This seems dumb. You only have to look around your friends to see that their eyes are all kinds of different colours: blue, green, brown, hazel — maybe even red!

True... but did you know them when they were babies?

⭐ And the truth is...

The colour of your eyes is decided by how much of a chemical called melanin they contain. Melanin is also in your skin. When it's exposed to sunlight, it darkens — which is why you get a tan during sunny weather. In your eyes, a lot of melanin makes brown, or even black, eyes. Less melanin equals grey, green or pale brown. The least amount of melanin leads to blue eyes. Because newborn babies have never had their eye melanin exposed to the sun, it hasn't darkened. So nearly all babies *do* have blue eyes.

There's an exception, though. Albinos are pale people who have no melanin in their bodies. They sometimes have red eyes throughout their lives.

Verdict: very nearly true... but still

A human being is capable of eating 50 tonnes of food

In some countries such as the USA and Japan, competitive eating is a popular spectator sport. The contestants have a set time to eat as much of a particular food as possible. Some contests even have prize money!

One of the all-time great eaters is Takeru Kobayashi of Japan. Kobayashi has won the famous Nathan's Hot Dog Eating contest six times (though he's only human: he did once lose a hot-dog-eating battle with a Kodiak bear). He also holds several eating world records, including:

★ 58 bratwurst sausages (each in a bun) in 10 minutes
★ 8 kg (17.7 lb) of cow brains in 15 minutes
★ 9 kg (20 lb) of rice balls in half an hour

But surely even the great Kobayashi couldn't manage to eat a whopping 50 tonnes of food?

★ And the truth is...

Not all at once, he couldn't. But through their lifetime, the average person living in a wealthy country does eat around 50 tonnes of food.

Verdict: TRUTH

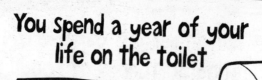

You spend a year of your life on the toilet

Actually, a quick trawl around the internet will tell you that human beings can spend anything from six months to three years of their lives sitting on the loo!

Obviously we all have to go to the toilet (on average about 8 times a day). But can all those little visits really add up to a whole year?

★ And the truth is...

Say you live for 80 years. In every four years there are 1,461 days. So forty years is 10 x 1,461, which is 14,610 days. Eighty years is double that: you'll be alive for 29,220 days.

Now think about how long you spend on the toilet. Eight visits a day, at an average of 4 minutes per visit, is 32 minutes per day. 32 x 29,220 (the number of days you're planning to live) = 935,040 minutes spent in the loo. That's:

★ 15,584 hours, which is...

★ 649 days, which is...

★ 1.78 years — or one year, nine-and-a-half months.

Verdict: **BUSTED** — it's actually a lot longer!

THAT'S TOTALLY GROSS!

Bleugh

You can assess your poo using a scale.
It's called the Bristol Stool Scale:

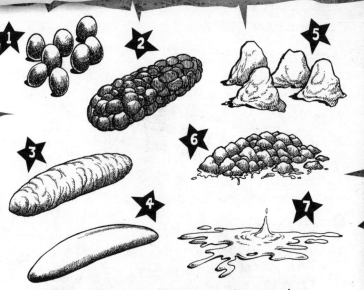

The healthiest poo types are numbers 3 and 4.
Numbers 1 and 2 show you're a bit bunged up.
Numbers 5, 6, and 7 show something has upset your digestion.

I'D NEVER HAVE KNOWN!

Here are three facts about body measurements:

- Your thumb is the same length as your nose.

- If you hold your arms out at 90 degrees to your sides, the measurement between the tips of your middle fingers will be the same as your height.

- From head to toe, most people are seven-and-a-half times the distance from the top of their head to their chin.

Computer keyboards are less hygienic than toilet seats

Imagine you're working on your computer, and a bit of food falls on to the keyboard from your hand. What would you do? Most of us would pick it up and eat it.

Now imagine you're in the toilet having a snack. True, it's a strange place for a snack, but imagine it anyway. A piece of food falls on the toilet seat. You probably wouldn't pick it up and eat it. It must be an awful lot less hygienic than a computer keyboard... right?

★ And the truth is...

A study by Arizona State University found that the average computer keyboard has up to 3,000 germs per square inch (6.5cm²). Meantime, the average toilet seat has about 49 germs.

This doesn't mean it's a good idea to eat off a toilet seat, just that it's NOT a good idea to eat off a computer keyboard.

Verdict:  TRUTH

Smoking makes your teeth fall out

Most people know that smoking is bad for you. It causes lung cancer and heart disease, among other health problems. Smokers die an average ten years before non-smokers. All that's bad enough — but are smokers also more likely to go through life toothless?

★ And the truth is...

Smoking reduces the flow of blood around your body. In your mouth, this means the gums receive less blood, so they are less healthy. This in turn makes it more likely your teeth will fall out. On average, smokers' teeth are about twice as likely to fall out as non-smokers'.

Lack of blood flow also makes it more likely that smokers will have to have arms or legs amputated (cut off) as they get older.

Verdict: **TRUTH**

28

You can clean a cut with maggots

Yeeew! This is the kind of thing you see in the movies, isn't it? Some wise old medicine man (or woman) peels the dressing off a deep cut to reveal a team of maggots, busy eating away the dead or rotten flesh and cleaning the wound.

Maybe it's something people used to do before modern medicine was invented — but surely these days we know better?

★ And the truth is...

Maggots are actually brilliant at cleaning away dead flesh from a cut or sore patch. They only eat the dead flesh, not living tissue. As long as the maggots themselves are clean, they do not harm the patient. While you're reading this, maggots are currently cleaning wounds in hospitals all over the world!

Verdict:

Mosquitoes like to bite some people more than others

If there are mosquitoes around, there's always someone who's covered in the itchy lumps their bites leave behind. If it's *you* that's covered in bites, there is nothing more annoying than someone else saying:

'Mosquitoes?
What mosquitoes?
I NEVER get bitten.'

Smells delicious!

So, is it just luck, or do mosquitoes really like to bite some people more than others? And if so, is there anything you can do about it?

And the truth is...

Some people do get bitten more than others. The main reason appears to be the smell they give off. Mosquitoes have very sensitive smell detectors in their antennae, which allow them to sniff their way to their favourite victims. Researchers think you are likely to be specially yummy to mosquitoes if you:

★ Have type 'O' blood.

★ Release a lot of carbon dioxide through your skin, for example because you are pregnant or exercising hard.

★ Have been drinking beer.

Unfortunately, apart from not drinking beer, there is very little anyone can do about most of these. Some lucky people do have skin that doesn't release a smell showing what blood type they have, and they are less likely to be bitten.

One thing to remember if you *do* get bitten is: DON'T SCRATCH THE BITE! It just spreads around the mosquito's left-behind saliva, and so makes the bite even itchier.

Verdict: _____

Foreign Accent Syndrome

This unusual and very rare condition usually happens after someone has had a brain injury of some kind.

No one knows why, but sufferers are left speaking their native language with a foreign accent.

Usually, sufferers speak with a Norwegian, Swedish, or German accent, but other languages have been recorded. There is no known cure for this condition.

Reading under the covers ruins your eyes

It's happened to most people who love reading. You're happily hiding under the duvet, long after lights-out, reading away with a torch in your hand. Suddenly, your bedcover is peeled back, and a grumpy adult who doesn't understand how totally brilliant your book is says:

'I've told you before, you're ruining your eyes. NO READING UNDER THE COVERS!'

Are they right?

★ And the truth is...

The adults are wrong to think that reading in low light damages your eyes. Scientists have concluded that it doesn't. Reading in low light conditions does cause eyestrain, however. This is only temporary, but can lead to itchy eyes, blurred vision and headaches. So put away your torch and go to sleep!

Verdict:  **BUSTED**

THAT'S TOTALLY GROSS!

Bleugh

The average nose produces about 200 ml of snot per day. You get rid of most of it without even noticing - by swallowing it!

When you have a cold, your nose really goes into overdrive. It produces four times as much snot as usual. The snot comes out almost as fast as you can get rid of it by blowing your nose.

In total, your body produces about a litre of mucus every day. Yuck.

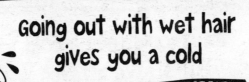

Going out with wet hair gives you a cold

'Put a hat on. If you go out/come home from swimming with wet hair, you'll catch a cold.'

Who hasn't heard this (usually from a grown-up trying to pull a horribly uncool woolly hat, knitted by grandma, over your ears)? So, are the hat-wielding grown-ups correct? Will going outside with wet hair leave you laid up in bed with the sniffles?

★ And the truth is...

Colds are caused by a virus, NOT by wet hair.

Viruses are everywhere and are easily passed from one person to another. The best way to avoid them is to make sure your body is in good shape to fight off an illness. Make sure you eat healthy foods, get plenty of sleep, and do some exercise.

Verdict: __BUSTED__

This is an age-old expression about how someone should be treated when they're ill. It means that if someone has a cold, but is otherwise OK, they should eat plenty of food. But if they have a fever — if they have a temperature, with hot sweats, cold chills and feeling groggy — they shouldn't eat at all.

★ And the truth is...

In 2002, medical scientists carried out a series of tests that seemed to prove that this is good advice:

The common cold is caused by a virus. Your body fights viruses using a chemical called 'gamma interferon' — and production of this increases after you eat.

Fevers, on the other hand, can be caused by bacteria. Your body fights these with a chemical called interleukin-4 — and it produces four times as much of this when you don't eat.

However, fevers can also be caused by viruses — so it's not always a good idea to starve yourself if you're feeling feverish. If in doubt it's probably best to ask your doctor!

Verdict:  half TRUTH half BUSTED

Laughter is the best medicine

This saying is used about someone who is down in the dumps.

'All he needs a good laugh. Laughter is the best medicine.'

But can laughter really make you feel better?

⭐ And the truth is...

Actually, it can — and not just by making you feel more cheerful, either. Laughing has several physical effects:

⭐ It makes you breathe more quickly, which means more oxygen gets into your blood. The oxygen helps your body to heal itself.

⭐ Laughing causes your body to release chemicals called endorphins, which not only make you feel better, but also strengthen your immune system.

In the 1980s, several US hospitals introduced 'Laughter Rooms'. Patients who visited them for 30 minutes a day experienced rapid improvements to their health!

Verdict: strange... but

BODY PARTS
THAT TELL
YOUR FORTUNE

'If the palm of your right hand starts itching, it means you're going to get some unexpected money.'

'If your left palm itches, it means you're going to lose money.'

These old rumours don't say whether it's the other way round for left-handed people. But it probably doesn't matter — before you run off to buy a Lottery ticket the moment your palm feels itchy, bear in mind that the whole idea is complete rubbish!

Your hair can turn white overnight

Imagine getting a horrible fright during the night (something even worse than remembering you've got double maths tomorrow), then waking up in the morning and finding your hair has turned white with fright!

There are lots of tales of exactly this happening to people:

⭐1 Sir Thomas More

More was an important advisor to King Henry VIII of England. He was also a Catholic, and when Henry decided to change England's religion and become Protestant, More objected. He was executed for treason in 1535. The night before his death, More's hair is often claimed to have turned white.

There is no evidence from the time that this actually happened. The story grew up after More's death.

⭐2 Marie Antoinette

Marie Antoinette was the wife of King Louis XVI of France. Louis was overthrown by the French people in 1792, and in 1793 he and Marie Antoinette were executed. Stories say that the night before her execution, when she realized what was going to happen, Marie Antoinette's hair turned white.

There is no real evidence for this claim. However, most of Marie's hair was cut off on the morning of her execution.

What probably happened is that her hair had begun to go grey months before, and cutting it short revealed the grey roots.

⟨3⟩ A.J. Littlejohn

Alexander Littlejohn was a steward on the *Titanic*, the luxury liner that sank on its first voyage in 1912. He survived after being ordered to row a lifeboat full of women and children away from the sinking ship. Photos published in 2012 seemed to show him with dark hair before the sinking, but white hair afterwards.

Mr Littlejohn looks considerably older in the grey-haired photo than in the brown-haired one, though this may have been the effect of his experiences. But the photographs were actually taken at least six months apart, so they don't prove his hair turned white overnight.

★ And the truth is...

Hair is mostly dead: the only living part is the tiny bit at the root, inside your skin. To go grey, it has to go grey in this living part, then grow out slowly. So, it takes months for someone's hair to go white.

Some people suggest that a rare condition called *diffuse alopecia areata* may make it seem as if someone has gone white overnight. It makes your hair fall out suddenly, and seems to affect coloured hairs more than white ones. If someone with a mixture of white and coloured hair had all their coloured hairs fall out, they would appear to have gone grey very quickly.

Verdict: __ **BUSTED** __

Alcohol kills your brain cells

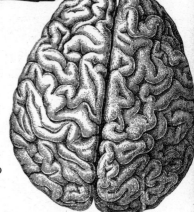

This is one of the sayings used to frighten people about the dangers of drinking alcohol. The theory is that alcohol is a poison, which kills your brain cells and will actually MAKE YOU STUPID if you drink it.

So — is there a drop of truth in this?

★ And the truth is...

Alcohol doesn't damage the actual cells in your brain. What it does harm is the neurons, which allow messages to pass between the cells in different areas in your brain.

Drinking a lot of alcohol regularly can cause permanent loss of neurons. The result can be problems remembering things, being unable to move your eyes, confusion, and inability to move smoothly and easily.

Alcohol also damages your heart, your liver, and lots of other important body bits.

Lots of bad things about alcohol, but on this one...

Verdict: _____  **BUSTED**

BODY PARTS THAT TELL YOUR FORTUNE

Want to know the future? Perhaps looking at your hands (or someone else's) will give you some clues. Here are a couple of old myths:

'Someone whose thumbs naturally bend backward will always have good luck.'

'A crooked little finger is a sign that someone will be wealthy.'

Sadly for those of us with bent-back thumbs or crooked little fingers, both these myths are complete nonsense.

Tiny creatures can take over your brain

There are loads of stories about insects or animals that can crawl inside your body, make their way up to your head, and slowly eat their way through your brain.

★ And the truth is...

None of the usual suspects, such as spiders, have ever been proved to crawl into someone's brain for lunch. But there is one creature that can do this. It's a tiny single-cell organism called an amoeba. This particular amoeba — *Naegleria fowleri* — lives in warm water. If you manage to get some of the water up your nose, the amoeba climbs along nerve fibres and into the brain. Within a week, the amoeba has bred and starts to eat the victim's brain. It is only a few days before the brain is so badly affected that the victim drops dead.

Verdict:

THAT'S TOTALLY GROSS!

Bleugh

There are two types of earwax - wet and dry.

Which you have depends on where your family comes from. People from China, Korea and the rest of north-east Asia usually have dry earwax. People from elsewhere usually have wet earwax.

Earwax might seem a bit gross, but it's actually really useful. Without it our ears would be dry and itchy. With it, they are self cleaning.

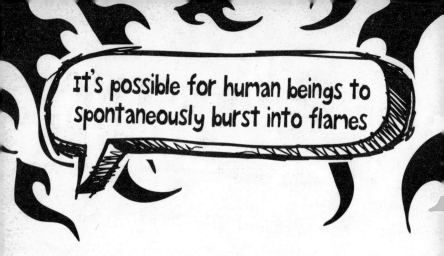

It's possible for human beings to spontaneously burst into flames

Down the centuries there have been many reports of people suddenly catching fire for no apparent reason. The victims are found with the area around them unaffected by the fire, as if their bodies have provided the fuel for the flames. This is known as spontaneous human combustion.

Until recently, most scientists would have said — to everyone's relief — that spontaneous human combustion is impossible.

★ And the truth is...

Recently, researchers have put forward a theory called 'the wick effect'. They suggest that in very, very rare cases, chemicals in the human body *can* catch light. The flames are then fuelled by the body's fat reserves. Wow!

Verdict: unlikely but JUST may be... **TRUTH**

I'D NEVER HAVE KNOWN!

You have a special muscle for kissing. It's called the orbicularis oris, and is used when you pucker your lips. Here are a few more things you might not know about kissing:

- The science of kissing is called philematology.

- Most people – roughly two-thirds – tip their head to the right when they kiss someone.

- The longest kiss ever recorded lasted 31 hours, 30 minutes, and 30 seconds – after which the kissers presumably fell asleep.

The human jaw is tougher than concrete

Concrete is among the toughest materials around. The Romans were the first people to build with it, 2,000 years ago. Buildings such as the Pantheon and Colosseum in Rome were built using concrete, and are still standing today.

Can your jawbone really be stronger than that?

★ And the truth is...

Yes, it can. In fact, *all* human bone is stronger than concrete. A block of bone the size of a matchbox can support a weight of NINE TONNES without breaking! That's four times as much weight as a piece of concrete could manage.

Your jawbone gets a special mention because it's the toughest bone in the human body.

Verdict:

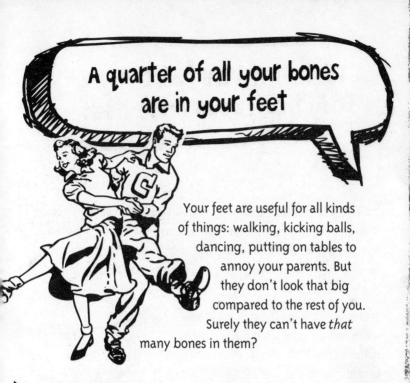

A quarter of all your bones are in your feet

Your feet are useful for all kinds of things: walking, kicking balls, dancing, putting on tables to annoy your parents. But they don't look that big compared to the rest of you. Surely they can't have *that* many bones in them?

⭐ And the truth is...

Fully grown humans have about 200 bones in their bodies in total. Of these, there are 26 in each foot, making 52 in total — almost exactly a quarter. The number of bones helps us make the constant tiny adjustments to our balance that allow us to stand up.

Babies start life with more bones — about 300. (As they grow, some bones fuse together, until they end up with about 200.) So in babies and young children, it's more like a fifth of bones that are in the feet.

Verdict: _____ **TRUTH**

A tooth is the only part of your body that cannot repair itself

Anyone who's chipped a tooth, or even knocked one out, knows that this is at least partly true. Once our milk teeth have fallen out and adult ones have replaced them, any damage to a tooth lasts forever (or until you can get a dentist to repair it, which doesn't count).

This is because the outer layer of your tooth is made of enamel, which is not living tissue. Once it gets broken, it stays broken. But is the tooth the only part of your body that can't repair itself?

 ### And the truth is...

If you are otherwise healthy, the other parts of your body can at least make some attempt to repair themselves. Broken bones mend, cuts to your skin heal — even your heart and liver can repair damage.

Like tooth enamel, your hair and the tips of your finger and toe-nails are also dead tissue. If you cut them off, though, they do grow back!

Verdict:

THAT'S TOTALLY GROSS!

Bleugh

The white head of a spot contains dead blood cells, body fluid, rotting flesh, bacteria and other debris.

If you think that's bad, consider the carbuncle. It's a boil (a kind of giant spot, deep under the skin) that has multiple heads.

In the old days, sailors were especially likely to get carbuncles, and the ship's surgeon would have to cut them out. Today they are usually treated with drugs.

You can have brain surgery while you're still awake

Have you ever watched an old cowboy movie on TV? If so, you probably have the idea that some minor operations — usually, cutting a bullet from someone's leg — can be performed on people who are awake.

This *can* actually be done, as long as the patient is held still, though it would be very painful. (In the movies, ten minutes later they can almost always walk with a slight limp, which would NOT happen in real life.)

Cutting open someone's head and poking around in their brain, though — surely not?

★ And the truth is...

The brain does not have any pain sensors. Once they have got through the patient's skull, the doctors are able to operate while chatting to the patient. This has been done to people suffering from brain problems that affect their movement. The doctor touches a part of the brain, then watches to see how it affects movement or speech.

Verdict: **TRUTH**

Eating ice cream can give you ice-cream headaches

Lots of people talk about ice-cream headaches. Not only ice-cream eaters, but also surfers, snowboarders, and people who like super-cold drinks all claim to suffer from them. But how could eating ice cream give you a headache?

In fact, if the brain can't feel pain (see opposite), how do you get *any* kind of headache?

⭐ And the truth is...

Headaches are not pain in your brain, although they do feel like it! They are actually pain in the surrounding areas, and are often caused by either too much or too little blood flowing to those areas.

Ice cream headaches happen when your body is momentarily fooled into thinking it is suddenly getting cold. This happens after eating ice cream, drinking a cold drink, ducking your head into cold water, or suddenly getting a blast of freezing, snowy air. The brain gets a message saying: 'Increase blood flow to warm yourself up'. Blood races to your head, and you get a headache.

Verdict:  TRUTH

You can tell when someone is lying

Imagine the scene. You go to the biscuit tin, knowing that three chocolate biscuits were in there earlier. Now there are none. Someone has eaten them ALL, not even leaving you one!

The prime suspect is your kid brother. But when you question him, how will you know if he's telling the truth?

★ And the truth is...

When people are lying, their body acts in ways that are very hard to stop. Clues to look out for include:

★ Touching the face more than usual, especially the nose. When people are lying, their nose swells slightly, making it itch.

★ Not looking you in the eye, or rubbing the eyes (which is just a way of breaking eye contact without looking guilty).

★ Answering your questions with the same words, for example: *'Did you eat the last chocolate biscuit?' 'No, I did not eat the last chocolate biscuit.'*

★ Jiggling their feet, shifting the lower part of their body away from you so that they are sideways-on, or not making many gestures with their hands and arms.

Verdict: ___TRUTH___

THAT'S TOTALLY GROSS!

Bleugh

People fart on average 14 times a day, releasing about half a litre of gas.

Farts are made up of gases including nitrogen, oxygen, methane, and hydrogen. They also contain small amounts of hydrogen dioxide, which is the main ingredient that makes them smell.

Some foods produce more hydrogen dioxide than others. Eggs, cauliflower and meat all lead to stinkers. Beans, though, make large amounts of gas but not much hydrogen dioxide.

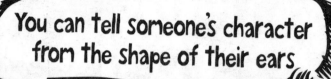

You can tell someone's character from the shape of their ears

Next time you notice someone has grown their hair over their ears, ask yourself why. Is it because long hair's fashionable at the moment? Or is it because they've got something to hide…

Here are a few things you can apparently learn from the shape of people's ears:

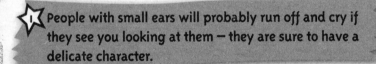

1 People with small ears will probably run off and cry if they see you looking at them — they are sure to have a delicate character.

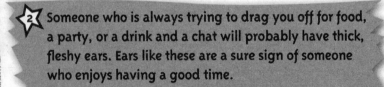

2 Someone who is always trying to drag you off for food, a party, or a drink and a chat will probably have thick, fleshy ears. Ears like these are a sure sign of someone who enjoys having a good time.

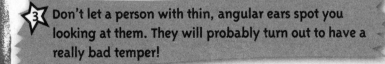

3 Don't let a person with thin, angular ears spot you looking at them. They will probably turn out to have a really bad temper!

4 Having long or sticky-out ears means someone is musical.

5 Have a look at the cleverest kids in class. Do their ears have big lobes? It's said to be a sign of intelligence.

And the truth is...

Most of us know that it's not right to try and judge people by how they look. Just because someone has eyebrows that meet in the middle, for example, doesn't mean they're stupid or stubborn. So it seems obvious that the same would be true of ears.

Actually, though, it turns out there might be a teeny grain of truth in this myth. When we are upset, tired, happy, or trying to attract the attention of someone we've fancied for ages, tiny changes happen to our faces. They swell or shrink in ways that other people subconsciously notice. These changes are biggest with our ears.

So, while ear shape cannot tell you what someone's character is like, there's a chance that a person's ears might be quietly sending signals about how they're feeling.

Verdict: ____ a teeny bit true, but really

Right-handed people live longer than left-handed ones

Apparently, left-handed people are likely to die sooner than right-handed ones. In fact, if you're left-handed your life could be years shorter!

The reason is that lots of the dangerous machinery we use, from drills to saws and all kinds of other life-endangering stuff, is designed for people who are right-handed. Because of this, women — who in general are less likely to use dangerous machines — are less affected than men.

★ And the truth is...

It's all true. Several studies have indicated that left-handed people live anything from 9 months to ten years fewer than right-handers.

Verdict: _amazingly,_ **TRUTH**

THAT'S TOTALLY GROSS!

Bleugh

Your mouth produces
1-2 litres of spit every day!

As if that wasn't bad enough, you produce enough spit during your lifetime to fill between one and two swimming pools.

Luckily, most swimming pools already have plenty of saliva in them, so yours won't be needed.

Male cyclists can't have children

This myth appears in the newspapers or on websites every few years, as yet another example of how Cycling is a Bad Thing (alongside: It's Dangerous, Cyclists Get In The Way Of Cars, and Cyclists Jump Red Lights All The Time).

The theory goes that there's something about sitting on a bike saddle for a long time that stops men's bodies from producing sperm. Without sperm, of course, they can't get a woman pregnant. So the poor male cyclists are doomed to a life without children.

★ And the truth is...

This myth grew up from a study of top-level triathletes (not cyclists) from the 1990s. Since then, no evidence that it is true has been discovered. In fact, it's more likely that cycling *helps* men have children, since being fitter is known to make conceiving children more likely.

Verdict: **BUSTED**

Fresh urine is cleaner than spit

Healthy wee has been cleaned by your kidneys, so the moment it comes out of your body it is sterile. Once it has been in contact with the air for a short time, bacteria start to gather and this is no longer so. But fresh wee is actually very clean.

Spit, on the other hand, is full of all sorts of yukky things. Mainly it contains water, but there's also stuff that fights bacteria, stops your mouth from being too acid, and lubricates your digestion. There are also bacteria from your teeth and the lining of your mouth.

And the truth is...

In the sense that only spit contains bacteria, while wee doesn't, fresh wee is indeed cleaner.

Verdict: **TRUTH** (just about)

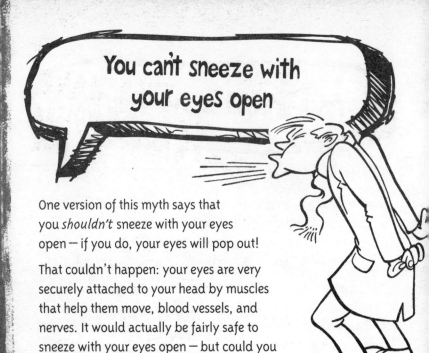

You can't sneeze with your eyes open

One version of this myth says that you *shouldn't* sneeze with your eyes open — if you do, your eyes will pop out!

That couldn't happen: your eyes are very securely attached to your head by muscles that help them move, blood vessels, and nerves. It would actually be fairly safe to sneeze with your eyes open — but could you do it, even if you wanted to?

⭐ And the truth is...

To answer this, you need to understand what happens when you sneeze. Sneezes are caused by something alien, such as dust or pollen, entering your nose. The body goes into autopilot, and expels a massive gust of air to get rid of the intruder. It expels this air by contracting muscles. As these muscles contract, so do the ones around your eyes. There's no definite reason for it — they just do.

As if to prove that it's not necessary for your eyes to close during a sneeze, some people are able to keep theirs open.

Verdict: __ **BUSTED** __

I'D NEVER HAVE KNOWN!

Here are three more sneeze-related myths:

- In ancient times, people thought that human souls were made of air. They worried that if you sneezed too hard and too often, your soul could be blown away!

- Saying 'God bless you' or 'Bless you' when people sneeze started in the Middle Ages. Back then, sneezing sometimes signalled the start of an illness that could kill you!

- Today, some people believe that their heart stops during a sneeze. Don't worry, it doesn't!

If you pull out one grey hair, two grow in its place

If you're reading this, it will probably be a long time until you have any grey hairs. Most people start to go grey in their 40s or 50s, or sometimes later.

Some people are so worried by the sight of grey hairs that they're tempted to pull them out. The thing that stops them is the myth that if you pull one out, two will grow in its place.

★ And the truth is...

Hairs grow out of hair follicles, tiny holes in the skin of your head. Only one hair can grow out of each follicle. If you pull it out, only one hair can grow out of the follicle to replace the pulled one.

What caused this myth to appear is probably that while the new grey hair is growing out to replace the old one, the hairs growing out of other follicles beside it have started to go grey, too.

Verdict: __ **BUSTED** __

I'D NEVER HAVE KNOWN!

Here are some facts about people with <u>blonde hair</u>:

- Blonde people have more hair than anyone else. They typically have 140,000 hair follicles. The average across all hair colours is 100,000.

- Only between 1% and 6% of the world's population is blonde. The only hair colour less common is red.

- In ancient Rome, women used to dye their hair blonde using pigeon poo. Other unusual hair dyes from history include black walnut shells, the spice turmeric and leeks.

Wearing hats makes men go bald

There's a neat variation of this myth that says a man who wears a hat *indoors* will go bald. The variation dates from a time when most men wore hats, and it was considered very

rude for a man to wear one indoors. It's not clear
in this version whether the baldness is the result of hat wearing,
or a punishment for rudeness.

Either way, is it time for all males to hang up their hats? (The
ones who don't want to turn into baldies, that is.)

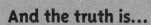

★ And the truth is...

The only thing that can stop hair growing is if your hair
follicles are damaged. When men go bald, it is almost
always because their body has started to release a
chemical that slowly damages the hair follicles. Whether
this happens to you is dependent on the genes you
inherit from your parents. It has nothing to do with
wearing hats.

Verdict: **BUSTED**

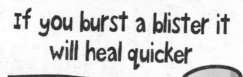

If you burst a blister it will heal quicker

You've been out to the roller disco/ skate park/mall in your new shoes. You get home, peel off your socks, and there it is — a lovely big blister! Right on your toe or heel. You poke it, you prod it, you give it a bit of a squeeze. Then you remember that someone, somewhere once told you that blisters heal quicker if you burst them.

It's so tempting — but will bursting it actually help?

★ And the truth is...

The skin over a blister is a natural protection against the flesh beneath getting infected. Once new skin has grown underneath it, the old skin of the blister will flake off. The new skin grows at the same speed whether the blister has been burst or not. And breaking the skin could allow an infection to begin.

Verdict: ___ **BUSTED** ___

I'D NEVER HAVE KNOWN!

Here are some amazing facts about identical twins:

- Every single person on Earth has their own unique smell – except identical twins.

- Twins start playing with each other before they are even born.

- The largest twins ever born weighed a total of 12.6 kg (27lb 12oz). They were born in Arkansas, USA in 1924.

- Identical twins are the only people who have the exact-same DNA. But their fingerprints are different.

snoring can be as loud as a road drill

If you have ever slept in the next-door tent to a snorer, you will know that some people snore really, really loudly. You turn over, you wrap your pillow round your head; you stick your fingers into your ears. But NOTHING keeps the noise out.

Even so — can snoring really be as loud as a road drill?

★ And the truth is...

Britain's official loudest snorer has been measured snoring at 111.6 decibels. That may not mean much to you, but it's about 10% louder than a road drill. It's also louder than a passing tractor, a moving train, or even a low-flying jet plane!

Verdict:

Eating bogeys is bad for you

We all know someone who's prone to a bit of *mucophagy* (that's the technical name for bogey eating). When they think no one's looking they have a rummage around with their finger (the technical name for doing this is *rhinotillexis*). If they find something juicy, they pop it in, give it a chew, and swallow.

Revolting, certainly — but is it actually bad for you?

 And the truth is...

One Austrian doctor has become famous for suggesting that it's a *good* idea for children to eat their bogeys. The rest of the medical world, though, doesn't really agree with him. Bogeys contain things that have been trapped by your nose hairs to stop them getting into your body. Eating bogeys allows them in after all!

Plus, picking your nose with your finger introduces bacteria, and can cause a life-threatening condition called 'cavernous sinus thrombosis'.

Verdict: Sadly (if you're into mucophagy),  TRUTH

Some of your body parts have no function and are useless

From time to time you'll hear people say that some bits of our bodies have no function and therefore we could do without them. The one that gets mentioned most often is the appendix, but there are plenty of others.

But just how 'useless' are these body parts?

⭐ The appendix

The appendix is a little pouch attached to your intestine. Up to one in 20 people has had their appendix removed, and it doesn't seem to do them much harm. One study did find, though, that the appendix is home to bacteria that help the body to fight some illnesses.

Verdict: May not be completely useless

⭐ The tailbone

Otherwise known as the coccyx, the tailbone is the remnant of the tails our ancestors once used for balance. Now that we're used to walking on our hind legs, we don't really need tails any more.

Verdict: Definitely not needed

⭐3 Male nipples

Why do men need nipples? The simple answer is that they don't. They have them because all foetuses start life the same way, and only later become either male or female. Nipples are one of things that develop before the foetus's sex has developed, so we all get them.

Verdict: Less use than a chocolate teapot

⭐4 Wisdom teeth

Human jaws were once a lot bigger than they are today. They needed more teeth to fill them up! Sadly, though our jaws are now smaller, the number of teeth in them has stayed the same. These days, the only purpose of wisdom teeth is to give dentists work, pulling them out so that our mouths aren't too crowded.

Verdict: Good for keeping dentists busy, otherwise useless

⭐5 Body hair

Back in prehistoric times, we needed body hair to keep us warm, and were covered in the stuff. Now, though, we've invented clothes and central heating, and the body hair doesn't really have a job any more.

Verdict: No longer required, except maybe for polar explorers

Overall Verdict: mostly  TRUTH

Intelligent people have bigger brains

In films and cartoons, intelligent people do often seem to have great big heads, bulging out at the front. Is it because their massive brains grew so big that their skull needed to be big enough to contain it?

⭐ And the truth is...

Someone with what looks like a big head usually just has a receding hairline. As the hair disappears and exposes more skin, the person's head *looks* bigger — but it isn't.

In fact, the size of your brain has almost nothing to do with how intelligent you are. For example Albert Einstein, who no one ever said was stupid, had a completely normal-sized brain. So do most of the super-intelligent people whose brain size has been measured.

Verdict: __ **BUSTED** __

> You can be so scared, the hairs on the back of your neck stand up

Have you ever imagined a ghost creeping up behind you? Strange noises in the undergrowth as you walk through a dark wood? Thinking about the prospect of having to go back and re-do a whole year of maths lessons? 'I was so scared, the hairs on the back of my neck stood up.' Lots of people use this expression to describe a spooky or frightening experience.

But do they *really* stand up?

 ## And the truth is...

It's not only the hairs on the back of your neck. ALL your body hairs stand up when you feel under threat or frightened.

It's a leftover from prehistoric days, when hairy humans lived in the wild, surrounded by predators. If danger threatened, their hair automatically stood up, to make the humans look bigger and more threatening.

Verdict:

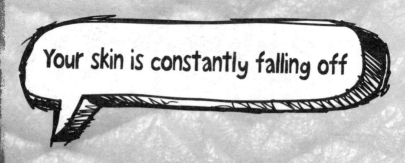

Your skin is constantly falling off

What a thought!

Just imagine what you would look like without your skin. Your insides would fall out, for a start. Surely it's your skin that's holding them all in? Without skin, you'd look like a meatball wrap without its wrapping or a chorizo sausage without its skin.

In other words, you would be just a shapeless lump of meat.

 And the truth is...

Ok, maybe your *entire* skin isn't constantly falling off, but quite a lot of *bits* of it are. Millions of cells in fact... Humans shed about 1.5 million skin cells every hour.

If you get a new bath sponge or flannel, it quickly fills with these cells. And not only skin cells, but also a common skin bacteria called *staphylococcus aureus*. If *staphylococcus aureus* gets into the wrong part of your body, it can make you quite unwell. That's why it's important that sponges and flannels are regularly washed.

Verdict:

THAT'S TOTALLY GROSS!

Bleugh

Sweaty people smell because of 'stink-bomb' bacteria on their skin

There's a particular type of bacteria that loves to eat sweat. As part of the process it releases a smelly acid. Unless it's washed off, this acid stays on your skin or in your clothes. Pretty soon you find people standing a bit further away than they used to, to get away from the whiff.

Sweat-eating bacteria especially like the sweat that comes from your armpits, feet, and underwear department.
That's why it's especially important to keep these areas clean.

We're only 10% human

This is actually true! Only 10% of the cells that make up 'you' at any one time are actually human.

- The rest of the cells are made up of the 90 TRILLION bacteria that live on or in us. They cover our bodies inside and out, from head to toe. You can find 20 million microscopic animals living on just 6.5 cm2 (a square inch) of human skin.

Head lice prefer to live in clean hair

Head lice, nits, cooties — whatever you call them, they are unwelcome visitors to anyone's head. They itch, they scratch, and if you're not careful they encourage their children to move to the head next door: your brother's, sister's, mum's or dad's.

Most doctors will tell you that keeping something clean is the best way to keep it healthy. It would make sense if keeping your hair clean kept the head lice away. But there's a rumour that the cleaner your hair, the more the head lice like it.

★ And the truth is...

Head lice are attracted to your head by the chance to drink your blood. Once they've settled in on a comfortable hair, they dig their mouth down into your skin and start sucking up a lovely (to a louse), warm dinner.

The louse doesn't particularly care whether the hair it's clinging to is clean or dirty. It just wants your blood!

 Verdict: **BUSTED**

Sugary drinks make you hyperactive

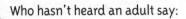

Who hasn't heard an adult say:

'No, you're not having another fizzy drink. It'll just make you hyper'?

What would it be worth if you could tell them they're wrong?

★ And the truth is...

In 2008, the British Medical Journal reported on the effect of extra sugar on children. It included fizzy drinks, sweets, and other sugary foods. The report found that children's behaviour was not affected by sugar.

What *did* change was their parents' view of their kids' behaviour. Things that would normally be thought of as 'just kids being kids' were suddenly blamed on sugary drinks.

The myth continues to be believed because children often get sugary drinks and sweets at times when they're also excited, such as Christmas.

Verdict: ___ completely **BUSTED** _

THAT'S TOTALLY GROSS!

Bleugh

Bad breath is caused by bacteria in your mouth.

Most of us know a breath monster or two. Usually it's someone who insists on leaning over you while they're talking and breathing into your face. Yeuw! What could be worse?

Well, try this: Bacteria live in your mouth and eat tiny bits of left-behind food.

As part of the process, they release a stinky gas. It's this gas that puts the 'bad' in 'bad breath'.

You're hot enough to boil water

Your body is one great, big energy-producing machine. It needs energy all the time, to keep your brain working, your heart beating, muscles working, stomach digesting, and lungs breathing in and out. If your body wasn't a great, big energy-producing machine, you'd very quickly die.

Even so, does your body *really* produce enough energy to make water boil?

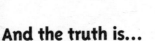

★ And the truth is...

Not if you're planning to plug in a kettle. There's no socket to plug it into, for a start. But in a more theoretical sense, yes. The average human body produces enough heat in thirty minutes to boil a litre of water.

Verdict:  TRUTH

THAT'S TOTALLY GROSS!

Bleugh

Poo is brown because it's full of old blood cells.

This isn't 100% true - actually, the brown comes from something called bilirubin. But bilirubin is produced when old, worn-out red blood cells are broken down by our bodies.

Poo is made up of about a third each of:

⭐ dead bacteria that used to live in our insides

⭐ fibre from our food

⭐ live bacteria, dead cells, and mucus that lines our insides and keeps everything nice and slippery

Brushing your teeth makes them stronger

This myth is spread by well-meaning grown-ups:

'Brush your teeth before bed/after breakfast. It will make them stronger.'

It's a bit like the myth that brushing your hair will make it shinier. That one's sort-of true: it actually spreads grease from your scalp all through your hair. Of course, the idea that brushing your hair makes it greasier doesn't sound as good...

Anyway, it's sort-of true for hair. Could it also be true for teeth?

And the truth is...

Keeping your teeth clean will stop them from decaying, but it can't make them stronger. In fact, brushing your teeth *too* much will wear away the tough outer layer, and make rotten teeth more likely.

The only thing worse is brushing your teeth right after drinking fruit juice. The acid in the juice softens the outer layer, making it easier to brush off.

Verdict: **BUSTED**

Here are just a few more of the many myths about teeth:

TOOTH DECAY IS CAUSED BY WORMS

The holes that appear during the early stages of early tooth decay look a bit like woodworm. Hundreds of years ago, people thought this must mean that the tooth holes had the same cause as the wood holes.

Fortunately, there's actually no such thing as toothworm!

WHITE TEETH ARE STRONGER THAN YELLOW TEETH

If the teeth are yellow because they're never brushed, this is true. However, clean yellow teeth are just as strong as white ones. In fact, artificially whitening your teeth can sometimes weaken them, so the yellow ones might even be stronger.

HAVING A TOOTH REMOVED AFFECTS YOUR EYESIGHT

This is a common myth: the internet is full of claims by people that after they had a tooth removed, their eyesight got better/ worse. Actually, the nerves and muscles that affect your vision are separate, and cannot be affected by tooth removal.

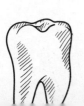

It's possible to be scared to death

How many times have you heard someone say, *'I was scared to death'*? Obviously they weren't scared to death — if they had been they'd be dead, rather than telling you how scared they were!

> Honestly, I was scared to death!

> Then how come you're still talking?

Is it just a saying — or is it really possible to be scared to death? Here are a few reports of people having died of fright:

★ THE OLD LADY AND THE ROBBER

In 2009, an elderly lady of 79 was at home when an escaping bank robber burst in. He was trying to get away from the police. Sadly, the lady was so scared that her heart stopped beating and she died.

THE EARTHQUAKE VICTIMS

In 1994, an earthquake hit Northridge, California, USA. Despite being physically unharmed by the quake, 20 people died when their hearts literally stopped beating. It seemed they had been scared to death.

DEATH BY SUPERSTITION

Superstition is a belief in something that cannot be proved, and which science says is unlikely to be true. In China, for example, the number 4 is thought to be unlucky. More deaths occur on the 4th day of each month than any other. The reason is thought to be that people who are already unwell fear death on the 4th because it is an unlucky day. It's the fear that kills them, not the fact that it's the 4th of the month.

In other countries of the world, people fear magic or witchcraft. When told they have been cursed or had a spell put on them, they feel terribly afraid. Some die — even though curses and spells have no real power.

 And the truth is...

Scientists have discovered that it is possible to be scared to death. When we are scared, our bodies produce adrenaline. This is a natural drug that allows our muscles to work far better than usual. But some people's bodies release too much adrenaline. It causes their heart to malfunction, and they die.

Verdict:

I'D NEVER HAVE KNOWN!

Every cigarette you smoke takes 11 minutes off your life.

That means a pack of 20 cigarettes knocks 3 hours 40 minutes off your life. Smoking a box of 200 will cost you a day and a half. And here are a few more facts you might want to think about before lighting up a cigarette:

- Smokers are likely to die about 6.5 years sooner than non-smokers.

- At today's prices, smokers spend an average of £78,000 on cigarettes.

Your ears never stop growing

If you ever visit an old people's home, or hang out with your grandparents and their friends, you might have noticed an odd thing. Those older people all have really big ears!

Is it because of something they used to put in the school dinners, back when the older folks were kids? Or is there some other reason?

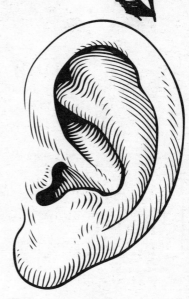

★ And the truth is...

At the age of about 40, you start shrinking. It happens because your joints wear down under the constant pulling down of gravity. Your ears, though, just keep on growing. (Actually, it's not only your ears — your nose keeps getting bigger as well.)

One bit of good news (if you happen to be female) is that men's ears grow faster than women's.

Verdict:  _____

Chocolate gives you spots

Spots — who needs them? What are they for? And why do they always appear right in the middle of your forehead before an important date?

Lots of people think that spots are caused by certain foods. The number 1 suspect is chocolate. But before you decide to become a no-chocolate zone (at least for a few days before the school prom), what are the facts about spots and chocolate?

★ And the truth is...

Tests show that chocolate-deprived spot sufferers have the same number of spots as greedy-guts chocoholics. However much chocolate you eat, the number of spots you have stays the same.

Verdict: 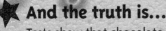 **BUSTED**

Here are some of the other popular myths about spots:

Spots grow on unwashed skin

The causes of spots are almost all under the surface of your skin, rather than on the surface. Although it's a good idea to wash your face twice a day, not washing isn't likely to cause spots.

Spots are infectious

Spots start to grow under your skin, not on the outside. Touching someone else's spots isn't much fun, but it wouldn't be likely to pass the spots on to you.

Eating greasy food gives you spots

As with chocolate, there is no proof that particular foods cause zits. It is a good idea to avoid greasy food, because it's bad for you in lots of other ways. But not eating it won't cure spots.

Sunbathing and sunlamps help get rid of spots

There is no evidence this is true. The myth probably grew up because having a tan makes the red swelling around a spot much harder to see. Too much sunbathing has been proved to cause skin cancer, though — which is much more serious than a spot that will go away on its own in a few days.

Verdict: ALL BUSTED!

THAT'S TOTALLY GROSS!

Bleugh

Your feet are the sweatiest part of you.

You have more sweat glands in your feet than in any other part of your body, even your armpits.

The sweat your feet produce is especially tasty for bacteria, which head there for a delicious meal. Then the bacteria release stinky acid, which makes your trainers really pong!

You need at least eight hours of sleep each night

'Time for bed – you need eight hours of sleep at least.'

How often have you heard this just as your favourite programme is about to start on TV, Grandma's sipped her Christmas sherry and is ready to do her special dance, or the football match has gone into extra time?

Sometimes it seems like this eight-hours-of-sleep idea must just be a grown-up plot to get kids out of the way before the proper fun starts.

★ And the truth is...

In general, adults do need between seven and nine hours of sleep every 24 hours. If you feel sleepy during the day, the chances are you're not sleeping long enough at night.

There are some people, though, who don't seem to need as much sleep. The former UK Prime Minister, Margaret Thatcher, was famous for only sleeping four or five hours a night.

Verdict: sorry, but it's basically  TRUTH

Where can I find myths about...

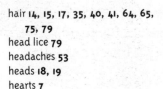

100%
SUCKER-PROOF

GUARANTEED!

Take a look at our other marvellously mythbusting titles...

Tip:
Turn over!

How NOT to be a sucker...

978 0 7502 8155 3

978 0 7502 6959 9

978 0 7502 6958 2

978 0 7502 8158 4

TRUTH or BUSTED
YOU SWALLOW SPIDERS IN YOUR SLEEP!
The fact or fiction behind ANIMALS

TRUTH or BUSTED
MEDIEVAL PEOPLE WASHED THEIR CLOTHES IN WEE!
The fact or fiction behind HISTORY

TRUTH or BUSTED
THE QUEEN LOVED TO SEE SHAKESPEARE'S BOTTOM!
The fact or fiction behind SHAKESPEARE

TRUTH or BUSTED
YOU CAN FILL SWIMMING POOL WITH YOUR SPIT!
The fact or fiction behind HUMAN BODIES

978 0 7502 7081 6

TRUTH or BUSTED
HUMAN BEINGS CAN GO POP IN SPACE!
The fact or fiction behind SCIENCE

BUY THEM NOW!

978 0 7502 7915 4

TRUTH or BUSTED
YOU CAN GET SUCKED DOWN AN AEROPLANE LOO!
The fact or fiction behind URBAN MYTHS

TRUTH or BUSTED
YOU CAN OVERPOWER A CROCODILE WITH AN ELASTIC BAND!
The fact or fiction behind SURVIVAL SKILLS

978 0 7502 8157 7

TRUTH or BUSTED
FOOTBALLERS EARN LESS THAN THEIR UNDERPANTS DO!
The fact or fiction behind FOOTBALL

978 0 7502 8159 1

TRUTH or BUSTED
BLACKBEARD'S HEADLESS BODY SWAM AROUND HIS SHIP!
The fact or fiction behind PIRATES

978 0 7502 8131 7

TRUTH or BUSTED
THE SMELL OF POO CLOSED PARLIAMENT!
The fact or fiction behind LONDON

978 0 7502 6957 5